TRAILBLAZING TEAMS
GROUPS OF PEOPLE WHO HAVE CHANGED THE WORLD

MARIE AND PIERRE

CURIE

WRITTEN BY

EMILIE DUFRESNE

DESIGNED BY

DANIELLE RIPPENGILL

BookLife
PUBLISHING

ISBN: 978-1-83927-357-5

©**2021**
BookLife Publishing Ltd.
King's Lynn
Norfolk PE30 4LS

Written by:
Emilie Dufresne

Edited by:
Madeline Tyler

Designed by:
Danielle Rippengill

All facts, statistics, web addresses and URLs in this book were verified as valid and accurate at time of writing. No responsibility for any changes to external websites or references can be accepted by either the author or publisher.

CONTENTS

Words that look like this can be found in the glossary on page 24.

MARIE CURIE

I was taught that the way of **progress** is neither swift nor easy.

Who was Marie Curie?

Why was her work so important for science?

What legacy did she leave?

4

Who was Pierre Curie?

What discoveries did he make?

Why was his <u>research</u> so important?

I am one of those who believe ... that mankind will derive more good than harm from new discoveries.

MARIE BEFORE PIERRE

MARIE CURIE

Maria Skłodowska, later Marie Curie, was born in Poland in 1867.

Her parents were both teachers and her father taught maths and **physics**. Marie was very clever from a young age, and was the top of her class throughout school.

She was not allowed to carry on her schooling in Poland at this time because she was a woman, so she moved to Paris in France to carry on learning physics and maths.

MARIE CURIE

PIERRE BEFORE MARIE

PIERRE CURIE

Pierre Curie was born in France in 1859.

When Pierre was very young, his father began teaching him maths and science, and he quickly became very interested in them.

After many years of studying, he began working in a <u>laboratory</u>. He did this to make money to pay for more studying and research. Pierre eventually became a <u>professor</u> of physics in Paris, and it was here that he met Marie.

PIERRE CURIE

A MARRIAGE OF MINDS

MARIE AND PIERRE CURIE WORKING TOGETHER

When Marie and Pierre met, they quickly bonded over their love for science and research. In 1895, Marie and Pierre married in France.

The couple went on to have two children, Irène and Ève. Throughout their lives, Marie and Pierre carried on researching. They worked together on many exciting discoveries.

Their daughter Irène also went on to study science as an adult.

RESEARCHING RADIOACTIVITY

Henri Becquerel was a scientist who researched <u>radioactivity</u>. Marie was very interested in his work. Pierre also became so interested that he dropped his own studies to work with Marie.

Marie Curie was the person who first used the word 'radioactivity'.

The **element** uranium had already been discovered. But when studying the **minerals** that uranium was found in, such as pitchblende, they discovered something very peculiar...

There were things in this mineral that had never been found before that were very radioactive.

EXPLORING ELEMENTS

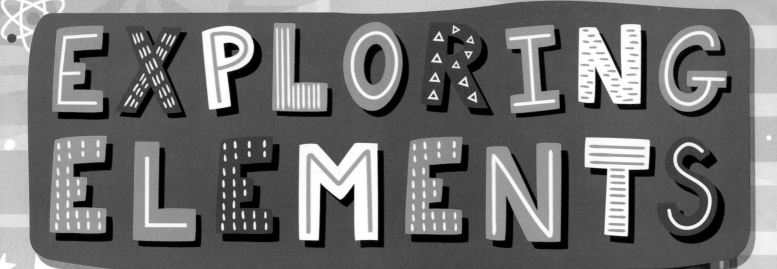

The couple soon began studying pitchblende very closely. In this mineral they found a new element, polonium.

Polonium is named after Marie's country of birth, Poland.

84 PO POLONIUM (209)

The Curies discovered another element, called radium, while studying pitchblende. Marie often spent hours in the lab separating radium from other materials, while Pierre studied it.

PITCHBLENDE

Radium glows in the dark. Marie liked to keep a glowing bottle of radium by her bed at night.

NOBEL PRIZE MEDAL

This award made Marie Curie the first woman to ever win a Nobel Prize.

NAT·
MDCCC
XXXIII
OB·
MDCCC
XCVI

ALFR· NOBEL

In 1903, a year after their discovery of radium, Marie and Pierre and Henri Becquerel were awarded the Nobel Prize in Physics.

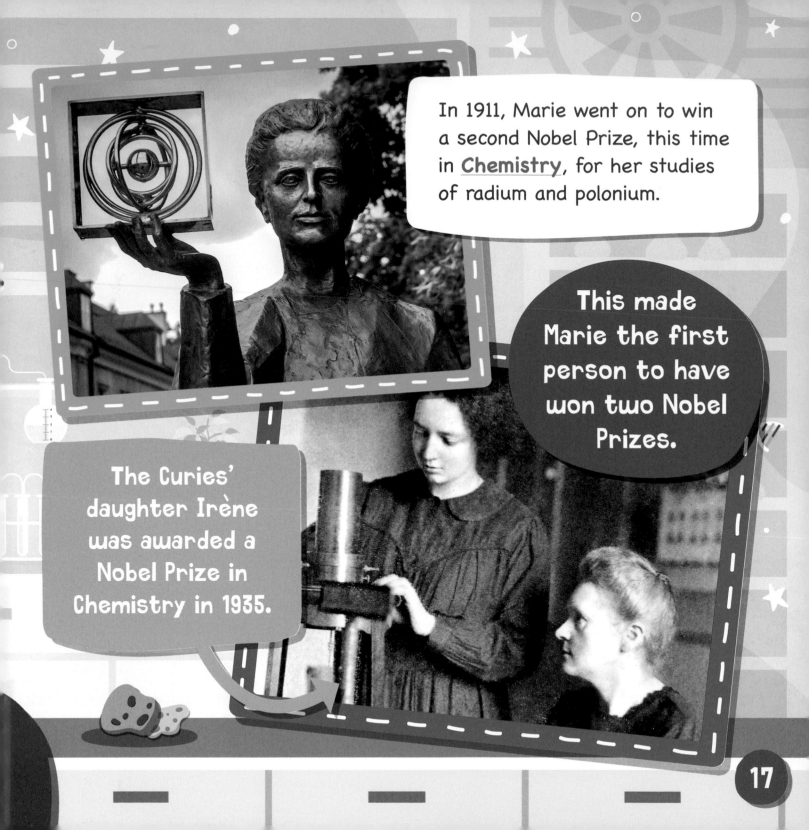

In 1911, Marie went on to win a second Nobel Prize, this time in **Chemistry**, for her studies of radium and polonium.

This made Marie the first person to have won two Nobel Prizes.

The Curies' daughter Irène was awarded a Nobel Prize in Chemistry in 1935.

AGAINST ALL ODDS

Both Marie and Pierre faced many difficulties throughout their lives, but they kept on researching and changing the study of science forever.

Marie faced many challenges for being a woman in science at this time. However, she did not let this stop her from following her passion for science.

Both Pierre and Marie faced money problems throughout their lives. They would work to save money so that they could carry on with their scientific research.

Pierre died in 1906, and although she was sad, Marie went on to continue the research they started together.

LEAVING A LEGACY

This person is having radiation therapy, a type of treatment for cancer.

Radiation can be dangerous, but when used in the right way it can be helpful. Marie and Pierre's work became very important in treating cancer, a serious disease that can make people very ill.

Marie made it possible for <u>x-ray</u> machines to be used on the battlefields during <u>World War One</u>. This meant that soldiers could be treated very quickly.

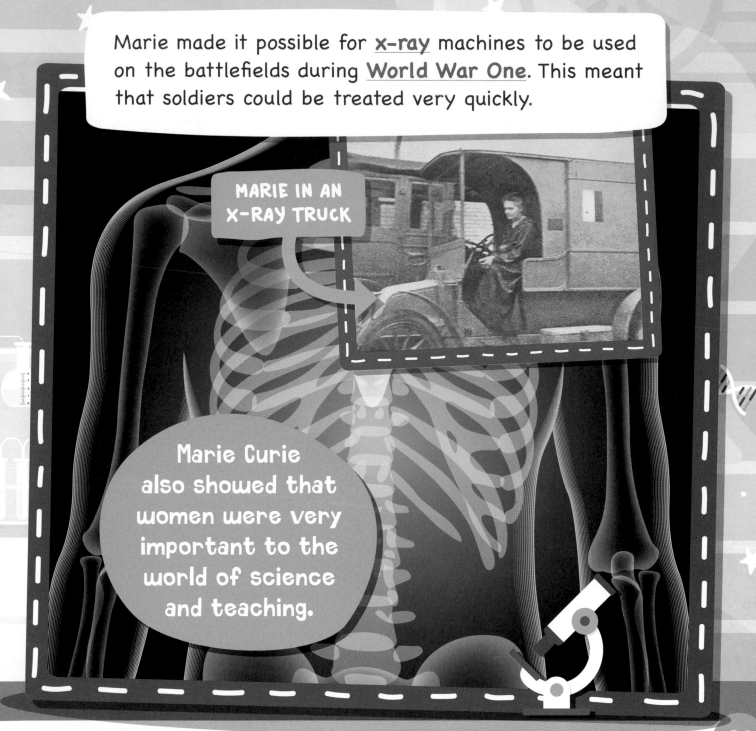

MARIE IN AN X-RAY TRUCK

Marie Curie also showed that women were very important to the world of science and teaching.

A TRAILBLAZING TIMELINE

1859

PIERRE BORN IN FRANCE

1867

MARIE BORN IN POLAND

1894

MARIE AND PIERRE MEET IN FRANCE

1898

THEY BEGIN RESEARCHING RADIATION

1895

MARIE AND PIERRE MARRY

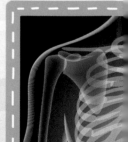

1903

THEY WIN THE NOBEL PRIZE IN PHYSICS, ALONG WITH HENRI BECQUEREL

1906

PIERRE DIES

1934

MARIE DIES OF A DISEASE RELATED TO RADIATION

1914-1918

WORLD WAR ONE

1914

MARIE BEGINS WORK ON X-RAYS

23

GLOSSARY

chemistry	a type of science that studies chemicals
element	a very pure material that is only made out of one type of thing
laboratory	a room or building used by scientists to carry out experiments and research
legacy	something left behind for people to remember you by
minerals	natural substances that are often hard
Nobel Prize	one of the most important prizes in the world, named after Alfred Nobel
physics	a type of science that studies the things such as light, energy and space
professor	a very important teacher in a university
progress	making important achievements which help the world to move forward
radioactivity	when very small things, called particles, give off energy
research	doing investigations and experiments to find out new information
World War One	a war that took place between the years 1914 and 1918
x-ray	a picture taken by an x-ray machine that shows the inside of an animal's body, particularly teeth and bones

INDEX